First published in Great Britain in 2005 by HarperCollins Children's Books.
HarperCollins Children's Books is a division of HarperCollins Publishers Ltd,
77-85 Fulham Palace Road, Hammersmith, London, W6 8JB

The HarperCollins children's website address is www.harpercollinschildrensbooks.co.uk

TheFA.com

1 3 5 7 9 10 8 6 4 2

© The Football Association Ltd 2005
The FA Crest and FA England Crest are official trade
marks of The Football Association Limited and are the subject
of extensive trade mark registrations worldwide.

Photography © EMPICS/PA except photographs on pages 16-17, 46-47, 74-75, and 80-81 © James Stevens 2004

All information within this book correct at time of printing, May 2005.
The views expressed in this publication are not necessarily those of The FA or any of its affiliates.

ISBN 0-00-721484-7

A CIP catalogue for this title is available from the British Library. All rights reserved.

Printed and bound in Spain

THE OFFICIAL ENGLAND ANNUAL 2006

HarperCollins *Children's Books*

INTRODUCTION

WELCOME TO THE OFFICIAL ENGLAND ANNUAL!

Inside you'll find profiles, facts and stats on all your favourite players from the squad as well as loads of cool poster pics. Once you know everything there is to know about the current team, you can check out the England and World Cup facts to find out the most capped players, highest goal scorers, youngest players, oldest players and loads more.

There are also loads of puzzles and quizzes to test your footballing knowledge. You can even design your own England kit on page 16.

We hope you have loads of fun with our official annual and that it keeps you busy right up until the World Cup Finals.

The England Squad

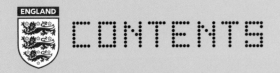

CONTENTS

DAVID BECKHAM

DOB: 02.05.75

Club: Real Madrid

England Debut: England vs. Moldova 09.96

Position in England Team: Midfielder

Appearances for England: 80

Goals Scored: 16

BIOGRAPHY:

Arguably the biggest name in world football, not only are the England Captain's crosses and free-kicks incomparable, his work-rate is second to none.

First capped at 21 by Glenn Hoddle against Moldova, Beckham's stunning free kick against Greece at Old Trafford took England through to the 2002 World Cup Finals and will remain one of the greatest moments in the team's history.

DID YOU KNOW?

Beckham has written his autobiography, *My Side*, even though he is only 30!

DAVID BECKHAM
England & Real Madrid

CROSSWORD

Fill in this fun footie crossword using the clues opposite.

If you get stuck, there are lots of clues in this book and the answers are on page 91.

CLUES

Across

2. Every international team wants to win this
4. Sven-Goran - - - - - - - - The name of England's manager
7. This is blown at the end of the match
8. This man wears black and plays every game!
10. England played this team to qualify for the 2006 World Cup
11. The stadium in which England won the World Cup in 1966
12. This card means you've had a warning
13. The wonderkid that plays for Manchester United and England

Down

1. England's badge shows three of these
3. He plays for Chelsea and England
5. He plays for Bayern Munich and England
6. The host country of the 2006 World Cup Finals
7. The colour of England's home shirt
9. Bobby - - - - - was captain of the World Cup winning England team in 1966
13. If you're shown this card, you've been sent off

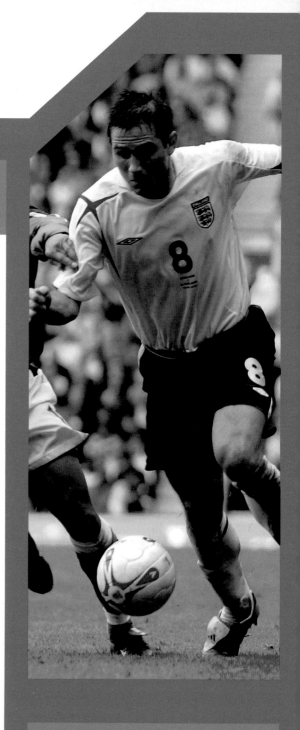

FRANK LAMPARD

DOB: 20.06.78

Club: Chelsea

England Debut: England vs. Belgium 10.99

Position in England Team: Midfielder

Appearances for England: 32

Goals Scored: 8

BIOGRAPHY:

Lampard began his career six years ago at West Ham, where his father, a former England full-back, was Assistant Manager. Lampard added an extra dimension to his game after joining Chelsea for £11million in 2001. He has become an influential figure, combining craft and tireless running in the Blues' exciting midfield.

On the international stage, Lampard has flourished over the past year, becoming a regular in the England side and capping a great season with three goals at Euro 2004. He was also one of four England players named in the official Euro 2004 All Star squad by UEFA.

DID YOU KNOW?

Lampard was named the Official England Player of the Year by fans in 2004.

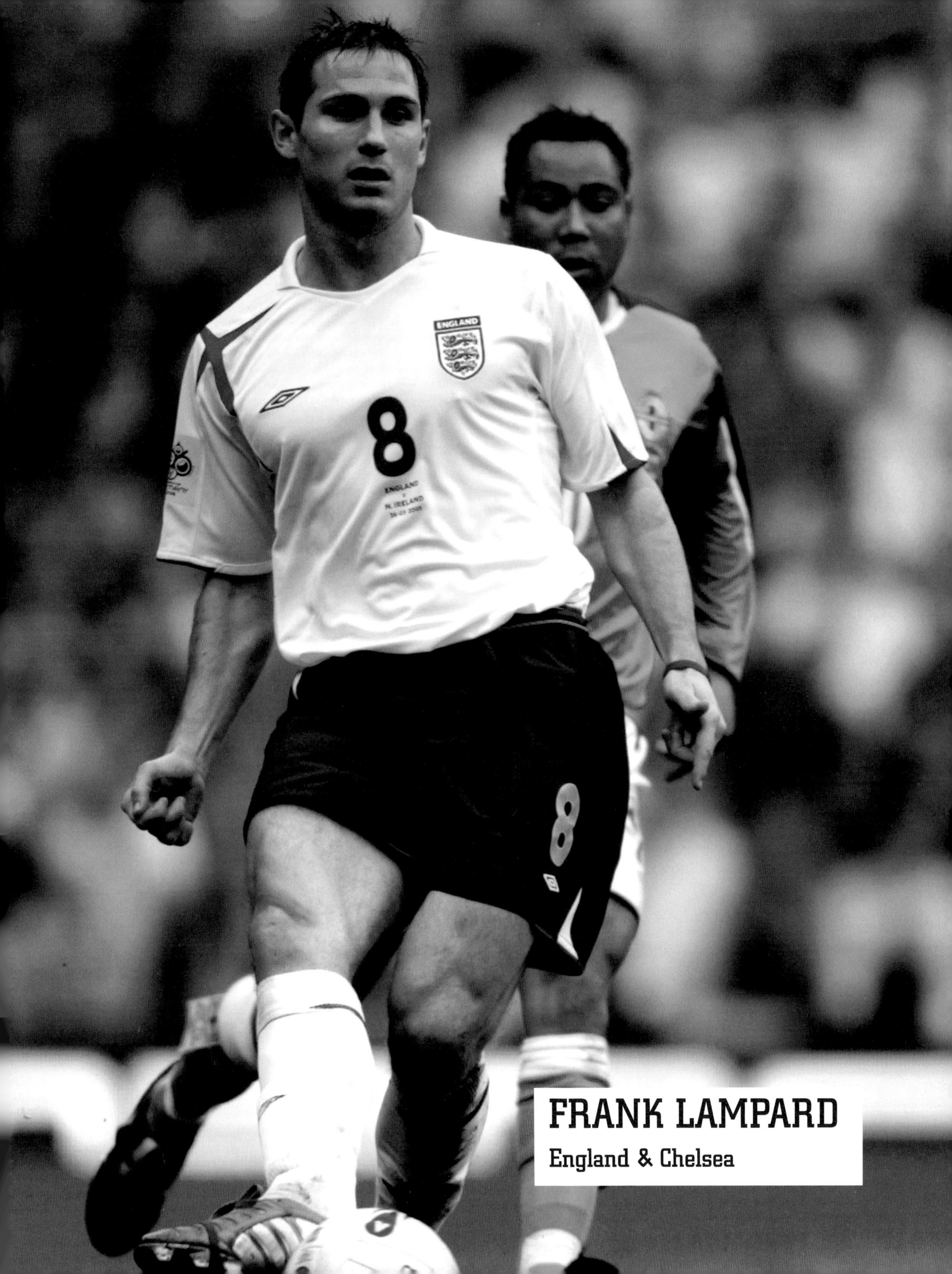

FRANK LAMPARD

England & Chelsea

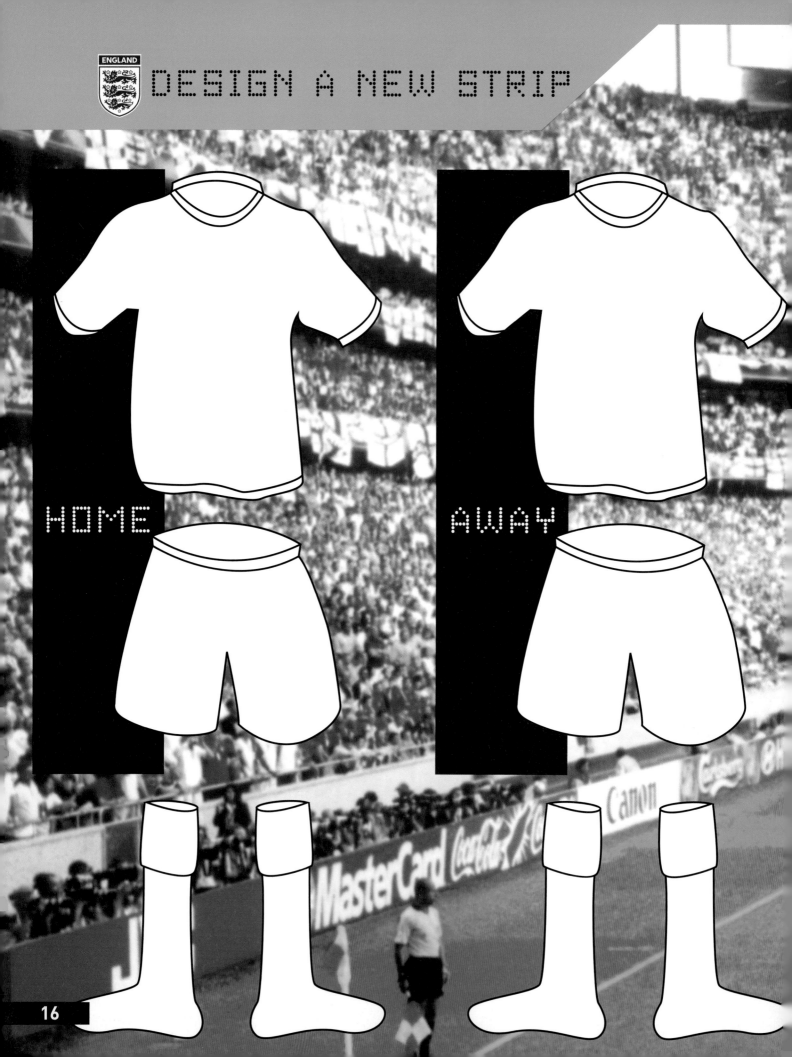

DESIGN A NEW STRIP

HOME

AWAY

16

TIME TO GET CREATIVE AND DESIGN A COOL NEW STRIP FOR THE ENGLAND TEAM.
They'll need a shirt, shorts and socks and you must feature the famous three lions badge.
Don't forget the goalkeeper!

GK
HOME

GK
AWAY

ASHLEY COLE

DOB: 20.12.80

Club: Arsenal

England Debut: England vs. Albania 03.01

Position in England Team: Defender

Appearances for England: 39

Goals Scored: 0

BIOGRAPHY:

With electric pace and an attacking instinct, Cole has added an extra dimension to England's left side. Though still young, he has been a regular under Sven and was ever-present in the 2002 World Cup and Euro 2004.

At the European Championship, Cole was praised for his performance against livewire Ronaldo in England's quarter-final against the Portuguese hosts.

DID YOU KNOW?

Ashley Cole was one of four players to be named in the official UEFA Euro 2004 All Star squad.

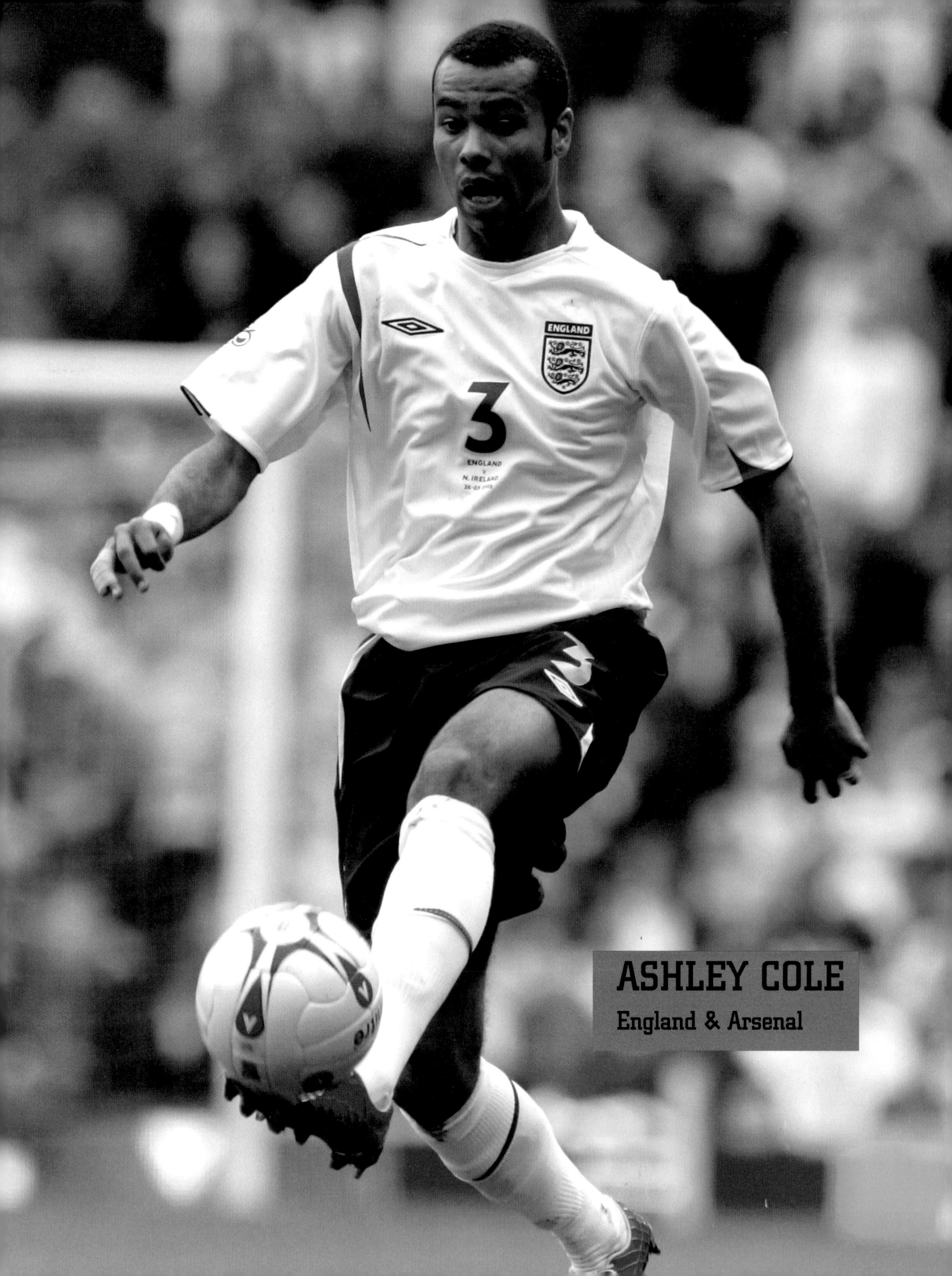

ASHLEY COLE
England & Arsenal

SPOT THE BALL

Mark on the grid where you think the ball is for both pictures. Answers are on page 90.

	A	B	C	D	E	F	G	H
1								
2								
3								
4								
5								
6								
7								
8								
9								
10								

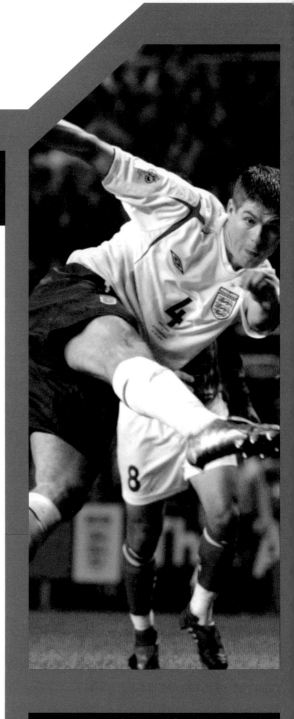

STEVEN GERRARD

DOB: 30.05.80

Club: Liverpool

England Debut: England vs. Ukraine 05.00

Position in England Team: Midfielder

Appearances for England: 34

Goals Scored: 6

BIOGRAPHY:

Skillful and aggressive, every fan, player and manager would love to have Gerrard on his side. He scores important goals for club and country – most memorably to give England the lead in the World Cup qualifier in Munich in September 2001 – and has a fantastic range of passes.

Gerrard was given the captaincy at Liverpool in late 2003 and followed that with captaincy of England, skipper for the friendly in Sweden. The Three Lions were unbeaten in his first 21 matches.

DID YOU KNOW?

Steven Gerrard was named PFA Young Player of the Year of the 2001-02 season.

STEVEN GERRARD
England & Liverpool

CAN YOU FIND THE NAMES OF ALL THESE FORMER ENGLAND FOOTBALLERS BELOW?

Remember, only their last names are in the grid.

Tony Adams	❏	Bryan Robson	❏
Gordon Banks	❏	Martin Peters	❏
John Barnes	❏	Peter Shilton	❏
Trevor Brooking	❏	Ray Wilkins	❏
Bobby Charlton	❏	Nobby Stiles	❏
Paul Gascoigne	❏	Teddy Sheringham	❏
Jimmy Greaves	❏	David Seaman	❏
Kevin Keegan	❏	Geoff Hurst	❏
Gary Lineker	❏	Peter Bonetti	❏
Stanley Matthews	❏	Peter Beardsley	❏
Bobby Moore	❏	Alan Ball	❏
Stuart Pearce	❏	Viv Anderson	❏
Alf Ramsey	❏		

U C B L D P T I M N E K N S K
F L L A E Y E S M A R E O R G
C A R A R S E A M A N E T E M
B H R E M N C D Y A B G L T A
M C A O K H E S Z Y P A I E T
E A O R R E N S E H N N H P T
N R H M L I N L Q D E F S S H
E O W G K T S I E J N J E B E
S E S L N D O R L S G L U A W
M M I B R I S N Z D I K G N S
A W V A O O R F N T O G D K Q
D P E G N R S E S Q C L F S M
A B O N E T T I H T S R U H K
B R O O K I N G F S A Z F K Z
S E V A E R G R P H G K O R V

JAMIE CARRAGHER

DOB: 28.01.78

Club: Liverpool

England Debut: England vs. Hungary 04.99

Position in England Team: Defender

Appearances for England: 17

Goals Scored: 0

BIOGRAPHY:

Carragher established himself with England's Under-21's, winning a record number of caps. The versatile player has made a number of appearances in the Senior set-up. He is one of the most committed and competitive players in the England squad. His determination was never more evident when he returned to action just four months after breaking his leg against Blackburn in September 2003.

DID YOU KNOW?

Carragher is a graduate of Liverpool's youth academy and was a member of the FA Youth Cup-winning team in 1996.

JAMIE CARRAGHER

England & Liverpool

JOHN TERRY

DOB: 07.12.80

Club: Chelsea

England Debut:

England vs. Serbia & Montenegro 06.03

Position in England Team: Defender

Appearances for England: 17

Goals Scored: 0

BIOGRAPHY:

Chelsea defender John Terry made his England debut against Serbia & Montenegro in June 2003 after producing consistently polished displays at the heart of the Blues' defence.

Like so many others, Terry had a great game in Istanbul, helping England qualify for Euro 2004. He returned from injury to feature in the European Championship, forming a partnership in the centre of defence with Sol Campbell.

He has since continued his good form, marshalling the Chelsea back-line and producing two vital goal-line clearances in England's World Cup qualifiers with Austria and Poland.

DID YOU KNOW?:

John Terry won the PFA's Players' Player of the Year award 2005. His team mate, Frank Lampard, came second.

CAN YOU HELP JERMAIN DEFOE SCORE?

Guide him through the defenders and be careful not to hit it wide!

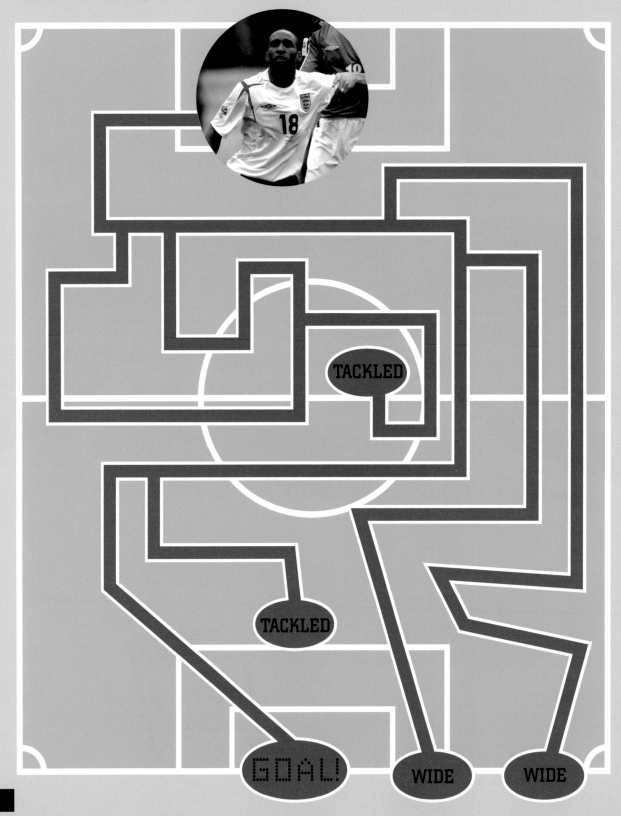

The first England player ever to be sent off was Alan Mullery against Yugoslavia in Florence on the 5th June 1968.

England's most regular opponent from 1872 to today, is Scotland. The teams have met 110 times and of these matches, England has won 45, drawn 24 and lost 41. The goal tally currently stands at 192 for England and 169 for Scotland.

The top ten all-time England goal scorers are:

Sir Bobby Charlton 49

Gary Lineker 48

Jimmy Greaves 44

Sir Tom Finney 30

Nat Lofthouse 30

Alan Shearer 30

Michael Owen 29

Vivian Woodward 29

Steve Bloomer 28

David Platt 27

Did you know, Wembley didn't become England's regular home ground until January 1966.

England's first captain was Cuthbert Ottaway in 1872

Peter Shilton is still the most capped England player, with 125 appearances for his country between 1970 and 1990.

SOL CAMPBELL

DOB: 18.09.74

Club: Arsenal

England Debut: England vs. Hungary 05.96

Position in England Team: Defender

Appearances for England: 64

Goals Scored: 1

BIOGRAPHY:

There are few more imposing players in international football than Campbell, capped initially in one of England's warm-up matches prior to Euro '96. He is now a mainstay in defence and a reassuring presence for team mates and fans alike.

His headed goal in the opening match of the 2002 World Cup finals against Sweden was his first for England, and he formed one of the tournament's most effective defensive partnerships with Rio Ferdinand. At Euro 2004, Campbell was again a commanding presence and was named in the official Euro 2004 All Star squad by UEFA.

DID YOU KNOW?

Sol Campbell was the first England player to be named in five consecutive major international tournament squads.

SOL CAMPBELL
England & Arsenal

RIO FERDINAND

DOB: 07.11.78

Club: Manchester United

England Debut: England vs. Cameroon 11.97

Position in England Team: Defender

Appearances for England: 38

Goals Scored: 1

BIOGRAPHY:

Ferdinand was first selected for England in a Wembley friendly just eight days after his 19th birthday.

Commanding performances for England in the World Cup three years ago cemented his status as one of the world's best defenders and led to a massive £29.1million transfer from Leeds to Manchester United.

Sven has always been one of Ferdinand's biggest admirers, while Harry Redknapp once described his as a 'Rolls Royce' of a defender!

DID YOU KNOW?

Rio Ferdinand was voted best-dressed man of 2005 by GQ magazine, knocking David Beckham off the top spot!

RIO FERDINAND

England & Man United

JOE COLE

DOB: 08.11.81

Club: Chelsea

England Debut: England vs. Mexico 05.01

Position in England Team: Midfielder

Appearances for England: 21

Goals Scored: 3

BIOGRAPHY:

Cole began his career with West Ham and from an early age, his extravagant skill and ability to produce the unexpected led to both praise and pressure being heaped upon him. However, he has taken it all in his stride and is developing well at Chelsea.

Cole scored a great goal against Denmark in November 2003 and his two impressive starts in March's World Cup qualifiers suggest that he could add a new dimension to the England team.

DID YOU KNOW?

Chelsea paid West Ham £6.6million for Joe Cole in 2003.

JOE COLE
England & Chelsea

CAN YOU FIND THE NAMES OF ALL THESE ENGLAND PLAYERS IN THE WORDSEARCH?

Beckham ❏

James ❏

Cole ❏

Carragher ❏

King ❏

Neville ❏

Brown ❏

Gerrard ❏

Hargreaves ❏

Terry ❏

Ferdinand ❏

Jenas ❏

Dyer ❏

Rooney ❏

Heskey ❏

Downing ❏

Owen ❏

Defoe ❏

Lampard ❏

Smith ❏

Butt ❏

Vassell ❏

Campbell ❏

```
T F L D F S B R T P S C S G X
J U E C R E E T E E H A M N C
Z T O R C A U M V Y D M I I N
D L N K D B R A A R D P T N N
E E H V M I E R A J R B H W P
W A F H V R N P E Z O E Q O L
M S F O G A M A P G O L P D N
L X A R E A S B N A N L H U W
N T A H L L Q S K D E I H N O
A H N E L L I V E N Y E T Y R
R E Q R A P M V L L S B R J B
C A R R A G H E R K L R C G N
C B E A A T A E E J E N A S E
E B H O J U I Y W T G N I K W
L C A Y X T I U O Q J S W R O
```

MICHAEL OWEN

DOB: 14.12.79

Club: Real Madrid

England Debut: England vs. Chile 02.98

Position in England Team: Forward

Appearances for England: 69

Goals Scored: 29

BIOGRAPHY:

A true jewel in England's crown, Real Madrid's Michael Owen has played a major part in England's fortunes since making his debut at 18 versus Chile in 1998.

A world-class striker with just under a goal every two games in international football, Owen's combination of skill, pace and ability to read the game make him a unique talent. He scored an amazing goal against Argentina in the 1998 World Cup finals in France and shocked the Germans with a sensational hat-trick in Munich in 2001.

With time on his side, the all-time England goal record is certainly within his grasp.

DID YOU KNOW?

As well as being a great footballer, Michael Owen is also an accomplished golfer.

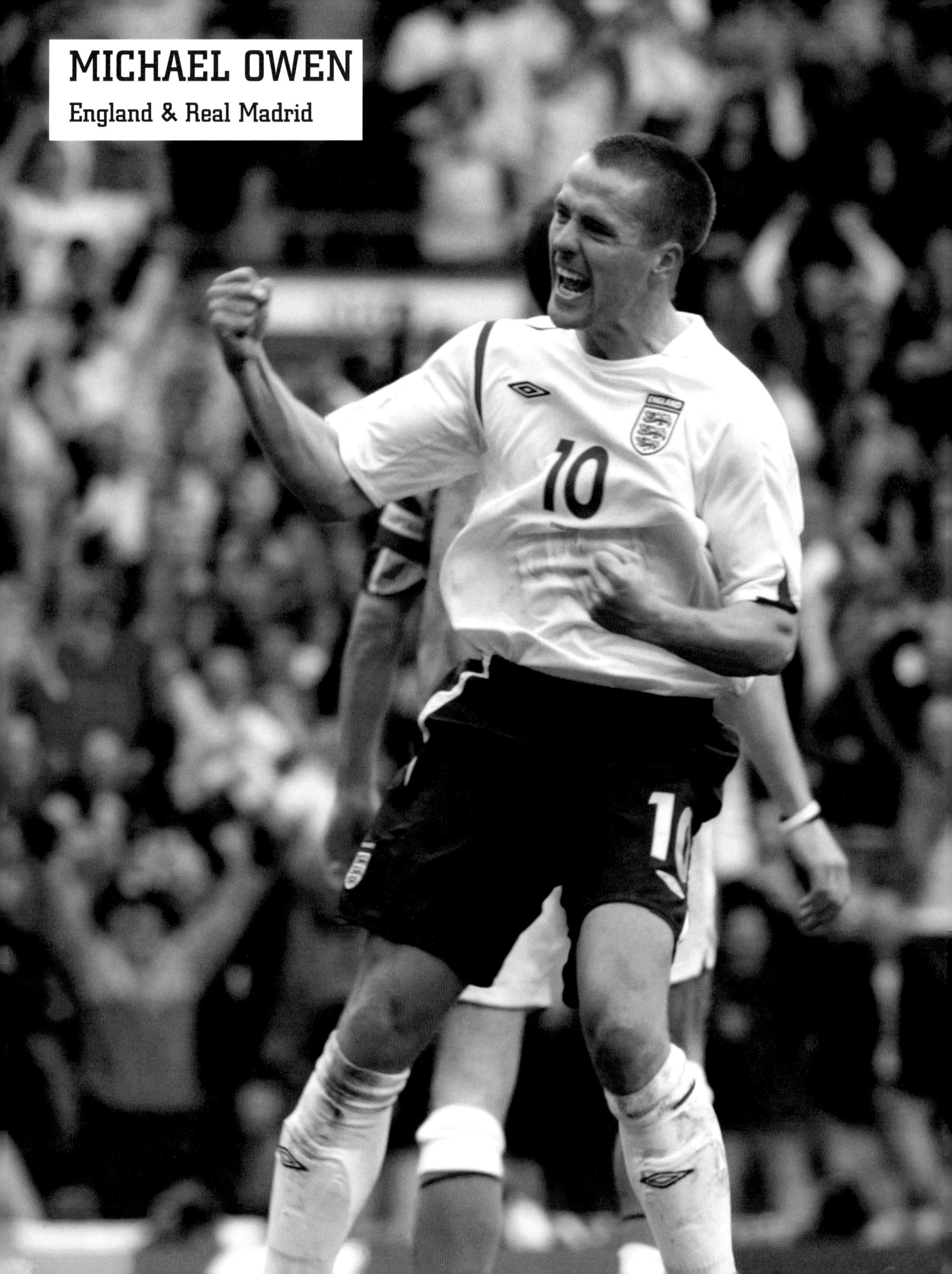

MICHAEL OWEN

England & Real Madrid

CAN YOU SPOT THE FIVE DIFFERENCES?
Answers are on page 90.

WAYNE ROONEY

DOB: 24.10.85

Club: Manchester United

England Debut: England vs. Australia 02.03

Position in England Team: Forward

Appearances for England: 23

Goals Scored: 9

BIOGRAPHY:

Wayne Rooney became England's youngest ever player (at 17 years and 111 days) against Australia in February 2003. One of the most exciting prospects England has produced, he is strong, quick, tricky and has a habit of scoring spectacular goals.

Rooney became the European Championship's youngest ever goal scorer, albeit briefly, when he netted the first of his brace against Switzerland in Coimbra. He went on to score two more against Croatia to become England's leading marksman of the tournament. These achievements were recognised by UEFA who included Rooney in the official Euro 2004 All Star squad.

DID YOU KNOW?

Wayne Rooney made his Premiership debut, for Everton, against Spurs at just 16 years old!

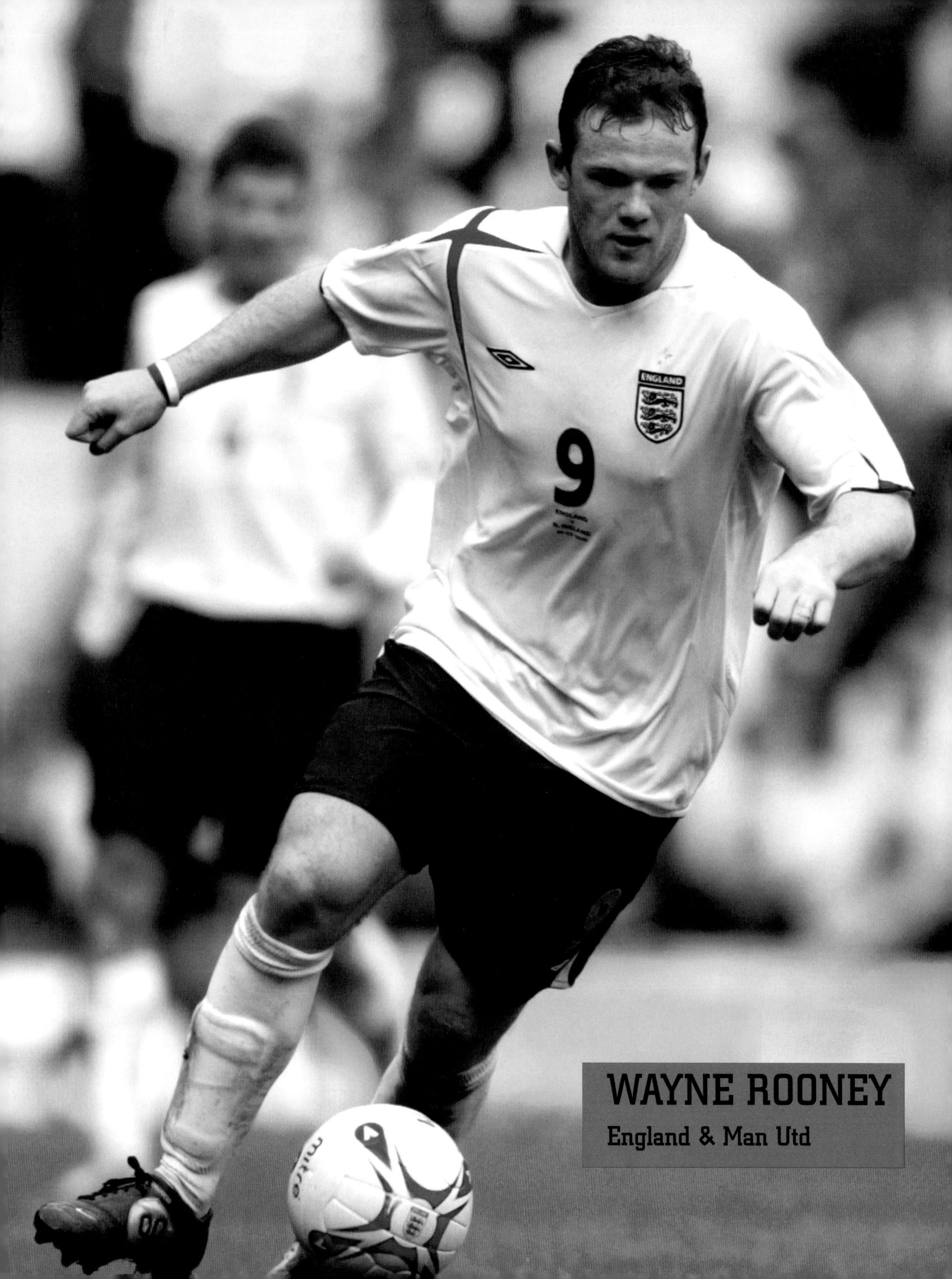

WAYNE ROONEY

England & Man Utd

5

4
GREAT TACKLE!
Go forward 2 places

3

2

7

6

1

8
FOUL!
Yellow card - Miss a turn

9

KICK OFF

10

11

12
FREE KICK!
Have an extra go

13

14

15
RED CARD!
Go back to Kick off again

Cut out the counters

ROONEY

BECKHAM

CAMPBELL

FERDINAND

INSTRUCTIONS

It's time for you and your friends to compete in your own championship!

This is a game for 2 – 4 players. You will need:

- A dice
- Scissors to snip out the counters. Be careful!

All players place their counters on the Kick Off square and take it in turns to throw the dice once. Whoever gets the highest score goes first.

Be careful not to get any yellow or red cards and watch out for that offside trap!

The first person to land on the Final Whistle square, wins the game.

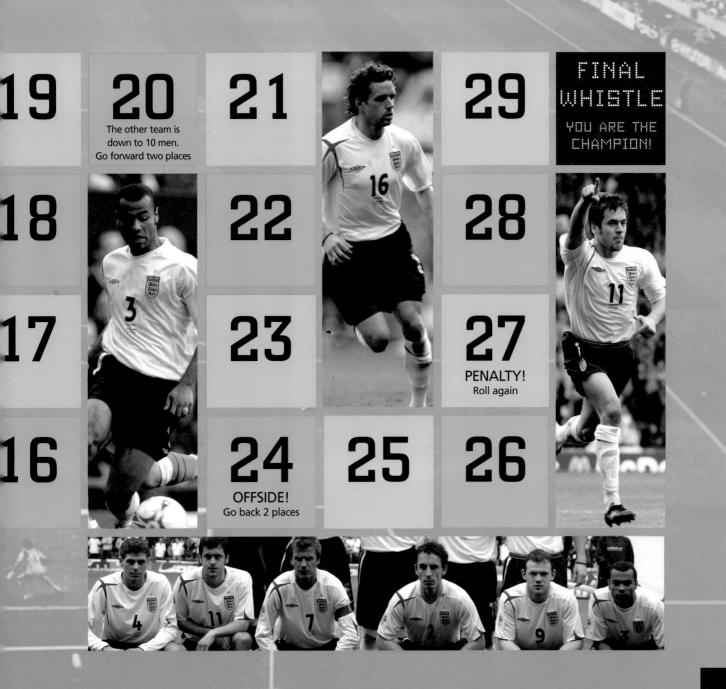

19

20
The other team is down to 10 men. Go forward two places

21

29

FINAL WHISTLE
YOU ARE THE CHAMPION!

18

22

28

17

23

27
PENALTY!
Roll again

16

24
OFFSIDE!
Go back 2 places

25

26

LEDLEY KING

DOB: 12.10.80

Club: Tottenham Hotspur

England Debut: England vs. Italy 03.02

Position in England Team: Defender

Appearances for England: 12

Goals Scored: 1

BIOGRAPHY:

Ledley became a first team regular at Spurs in the 2000-01 season under the tutelage of George Graham. He was soon tipped for the top and won his first full England cap in 2002 against Italy.

King was sub in that match but was given his first England start by Sven in early 2004. He excelled in the heart of England's defence, scored his first international goal and was subsequently called up to the Euro 2004 squad. There he started England's opening match of the tournament against France, and was highly commended for his performance.

DID YOU KNOW?:

Ledley King made his first team debut for Spurs at just 18.

LEDLEY KING

England & Spurs

JERMAIN DEFOE

DOB: 07.10.82

Club: Tottenham Hotspur

England Debut: England vs. Sweden 03.04

Position in England Team: Forward

Appearances for England: 10

Goals Scored: 1

BIOGRAPHY:

Defoe is one of England's most exciting young prospects. After being linked to both Manchester United and Arsenal, he finally put pen to paper with Spurs to return to the Premiership in January 2004.

His combination of pace and finishing has allowed him to continue his goal-scoring form in the top domestic league. Defoe will be determined to hold on to his place in the squad.

DID YOU KNOW?

Jermain Defoe put in an awesome performance in the World Cup qualifier in Poland, scoring a vital goal on his first full England start.

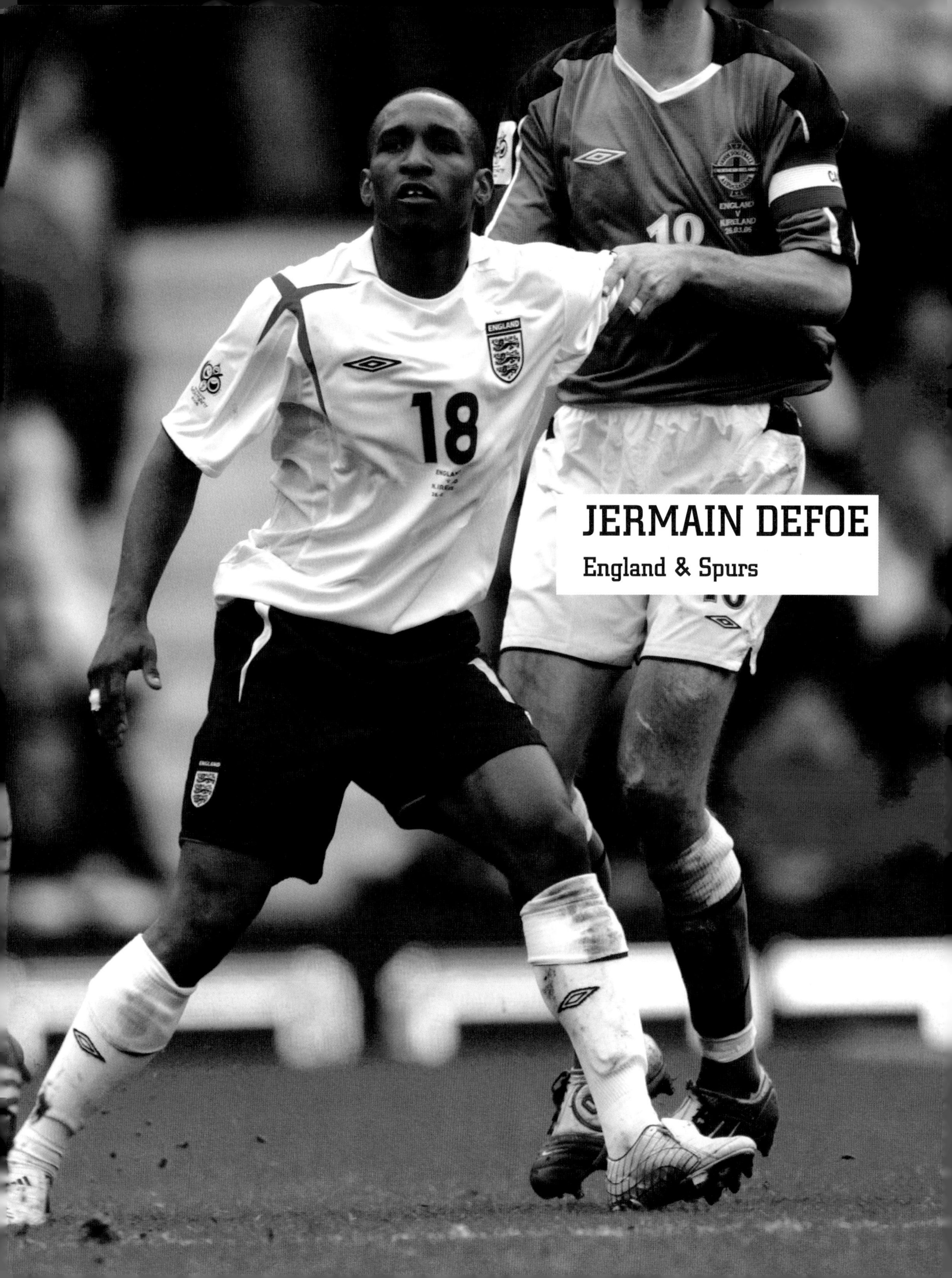

JERMAIN DEFOE
England & Spurs

KIERON DYER

DOB: 29.12.78

Club: Newcastle United

England Debut:

England vs. Luxembourg 09.99

Position in England Team: Midfielder

Appearances for England: 28

Goals Scored: 0

BIOGRAPHY:

When playing for England, Dyer is a frightening prospect for any defence and it can only be a matter of time before this midfielder with pace and an eye for a goal, really has the chance to shine.

Dyer received his first England cap at only 20 years old and the future looked bright for the Newcastle star, but so far, injuries have denied him the chance to fulfil his potential as an international player.

DID YOU KNOW?

Kieron Dyer is a great all-round sportsman and still finds time for the occasional game of tennis.

KIERON DYER
England & Newcastle Utd

Brazil has won the World Cup more times than any other team, with five wins.

England has won the World Cup once, at Wembley, on 30th July 1966 against West Germany.

The score was 4 - 2 and the England goal scorers were Martin Peters and Geoff Hurst, the first player ever to score a hat trick in a World Cup final. Hurst also scored the first goal with a header in a World Cup final.

The only footballer to play in the World Cup with one arm, was Castro, playing for Uruguay in 1930.

Brazil also top the charts as the team to have participated in the most World Cups:

Brazil 16

Germany 14

Italy 14

Argentina 12

Mexico 11

Over 1,100 players have been selected for England's senior international side.

England has played in eleven World Cup Finals tournaments:

Brazil 1950

Switzerland 1954

Sweden 1958

Chile 1962

England 1966

Mexico 1970

Spain 1982

Mexico 1986

Italy 1990

France 1998

Korea and Japan 2002

200,000 people attended the Brazil vs. Uruguay match at the Maracana Stadium in 1950.

The youngest player ever to play in the World Cup Finals was Northern Ireland's Norman Whiteside in 1982. He was only 17 years and 42 days old.

The oldest player was Cameroon's Roger Milla who was 42 years and 39 days old when he played against Russia in 1994.

In 1962, the Brazil vs. England match had to be interrupted when a dog ran on the pitch and England's Jimmy Greaves had to catch him!

Only one player has ever played World Cup football and World Cup cricket. It was Viv Richards who played football for Antigua and cricket for the West Indies.

England's World Cup winning team was made up of:

Nobby Stiles, Roger Hunt, Gordon Banks, Jackie Charlton, George Cohen, Ray Wilson, Martin Peters, Geoff Hurst, Bobby Moore, Alan Ball, Bobby Charlton and Sir Alf Ramsey (Manager).

SHAUN WRIGHT-PHILIPS

DOB: 25.10.81

Club: Manchester City

England Debut: England vs. Ukraine 08.04

Position in England Team: Midfielder

Appearances for England: 4

Goals Scored: 1

BIOGRAPHY:

Wright-Phillips enjoyed a great season with Manchester City in 2003-04 and earned his first call-up to the Senior squad to face Sweden, but never made it on to the pitch.

Wright-Phillips made his debut as a substitute in a friendly with Ukraine in August 2004. Not content with the new cap alone, he also produced a fine goal to help England round off a 3-0 win.

DID YOU KNOW?:

Shaun Wright-Phillips' father is former England player, Ian Wright.

JUMBLED WORDS

CAN YOU REARRANGE THE NAMES OF THE STADIUMS ENGLAND HAVE PLAYED AT?

Once you've rearranged the letters, match them up with the home team.

The first one is done for you.

1. enadfil   A N F I E L D

2. tranmpo dora   _ _ _ _ _ _ _ _ _ _

3. ts ymras   _ _ _ _ _ _'_

4. ts ejasm rakp   _ _ _ _ _ _ _' _ _ _ _

5. artmsfdo igdreb   _ _ _ _ _ _ _ _ _ _ _ _ _

6. ilvla kapr   _ _ _ _ _ _ _ _ _ _

7. ieirdevrs   _ _ _ _ _ _ _ _ _

8. dol raotdfrf   _ _ _ _ _ _ _ _ _ _

☐ Manchester United	☐ Aston Villa
☐ Newcastle United	☐ Middlesbrough
☐ Chelsea	☐ Southampton
1 Liverpool	☐ Ipswich Town

PAUL ROBINSON

DOB: 15.10.79

Club: Tottenham Hotspur

England Debut: England vs. Australia 02.03

Position in England Team: Goalkeeper

Appearances for England: 12

Goals Scored: 0

BIOGRAPHY:

For such a young keeper, Robinson has fantastic experience, having produced great displays in both the Premiership and Champions League. Throughout his career, he has proven himself to be a confident, agile shot stopper.

After managing to keep his form and composure during a turbulent season at Elland Road, Robinson completed a long anticipated move to Spurs in the summer of 2004.

He came into England's starting XI for the crucial World Cup qualifier in Poland and continued the fine form he had shown at the start of the season.

DID YOU KNOW?

Paul hails from Beverley in Humberside and has played for Leeds and Tottenham Hotspur at professional level.

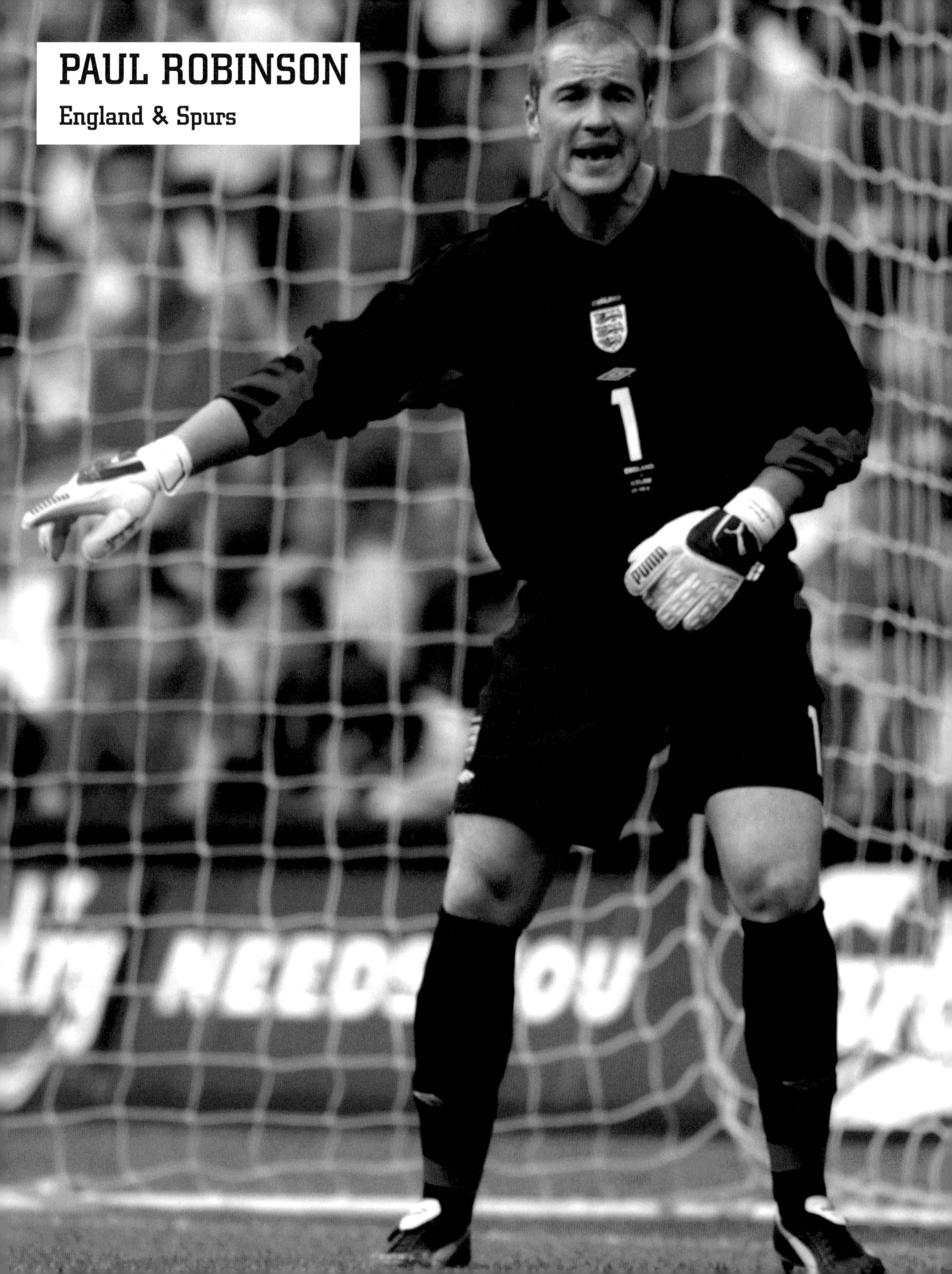

PAUL ROBINSON

England & Spurs

Can you crack the code to work out which players and stadiums are listed below?

1	2	3	4	5	6	7	8	9	10	11	12	13
A	M	B	T	L	P	N	R	C	K	U	X	O
14	15	16	17	18	19	20	21	22	23	24	25	26
D	J	Q	S	H	E	V	I	Y	F	W	Z	G

14	1	20	21	14

3	19	9	10	18	1	2

24	19	2	3	5	19	22

24	1	22	7	19

8	13	13	7	19	22

23	8	1	7	10

5	1	2	6	1	8	14

13	5	14

4	8	1	23	23	13	8	14

FOOTBALL JOKES

Which football team loves ice-cream?

Aston Vanilla!

What lights up a football stadium?

A football match!

What do a footballer and a magician have in common?

Both do hat tricks!

Where do spiders play their FA Cup final?

Webley stadium!

Why did the chicken get sent off?

For persistent fowl play!

How do you stop squirrels playing football in the garden?

Hide the ball, it drives them nuts!

What tea do footballers drink?

Penaltea!

What's the chilliest ground in the Premiership?

Cold Trafford!

When fish play football, who is the captain?

The team's kipper!

Why did a footballer take a piece of rope onto the pitch?

He was the skipper!

What are Brazilian fans called?

Brazil nuts!

DAVID JAMES

DOB: 01.08.70

Club: Manchester City

England Debut: England vs. Mexico 03.97

Position in England Team: Goalkeeper

Appearances for England: 30

Goals Scored: 0

BIOGRAPHY:

James won his first Senior cap against Mexico in 1997 and for a long spell following David Seaman's retirement, made the England keeper's jersey his own. James had two superb games against Turkey to help England qualify for Euro 2004 and moved to Manchester City to test himself in the Premiership once more in the run-up to the Championship in Portugal.

DID YOU KNOW?

David James is a woodwork-scraping 1.96 metres tall.

DAVID JAMES
England & Man City

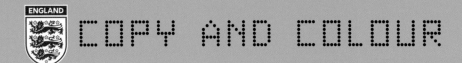

GARY NEVILLE

DOB: 18.02.75

Club: Manchester United

England Debut: England vs. Japan 06.95

Position in England Team: Defender

Appearances for England: 76

Goals Scored: 0

BIOGRAPHY:

An experienced England full-back, first capped in the 1995 Umbro Cup, Neville is one of England's most reliable performers. Not only is he a first class defender, his link-up play with Beckham down the right continues to be one of England's most effective avenues of attack.

He has featured in four major tournaments for England – Euro 96, the 1998 World Cup, Euro 2000 and Euro 2004. Gary missed the World Cup finals in 2002 due to a broken foot.

DID YOU KNOW?

Gary Neville was the 'best man' at best friend, David Beckham's wedding.

GARY NEVILLE
England & Man Utd

Mark on the grid where you think the ball is for both pictures. Answers are on page 91.

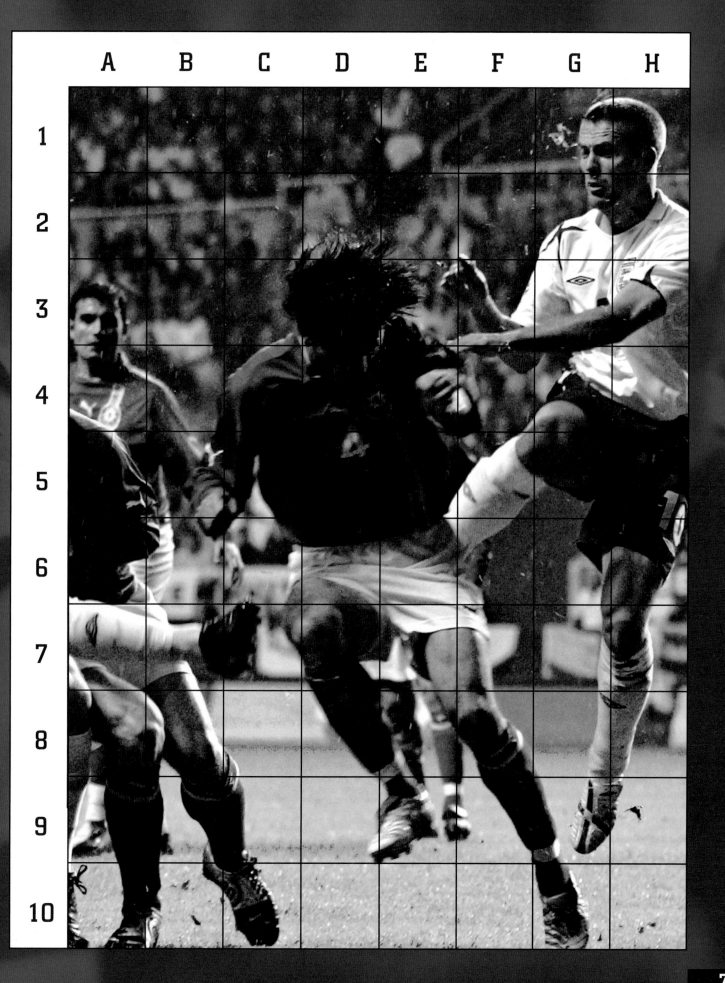

	A	B	C	D	E	F	G	H
1								
2								
3								
4								
5								
6								
7								
8								
9								
10								

OWEN HARGREAVES

DOB: 20.01.81

Club: Bayern Munich

England Debut: England vs. Holland 08.01

Position in England Team: Midfielder

Appearances for England: 26

Goals Scored: 0

BIOGRAPHY:

Hargreaves plays his club football for Bayern Munich and is one of the brightest stars in the German Bundesliga. He quickly graduated from England's Under-21s to the Senior team during 2001, making his debut in the friendly with Holland at White Hart Lane.

Initially appearing on the left of midfield, Hargreaves looks assured in a range of positions, including right-back. He's played in both the World Cup and European Championship finals and is renowned for being one of the quickest and fittest members of the squad.

DID YOU KNOW?

Owen Hargreaves was actually born in Calgary, Canada.

OWEN HARGREAVES

England & Bayern Munich

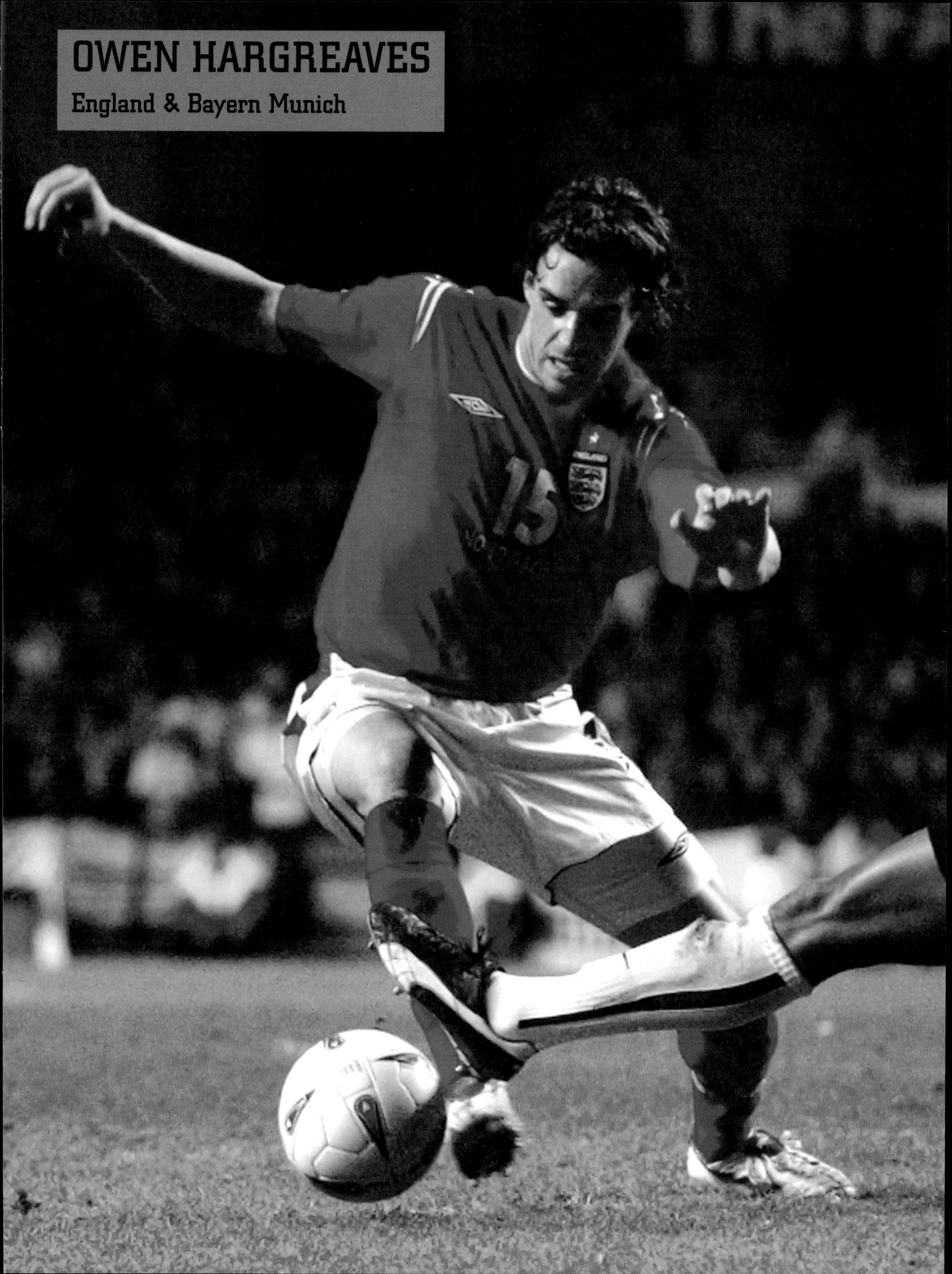

HIDDEN IN THIS WORDSEARCH ARE THE NAMES OF JUST SOME OF THE COUNTRIES ENGLAND HAVE PLAYED AGAINST.

Can you find them all?

Ukraine	❏	Switzerland	❏
Austria	❏	Portugal	❏
Poland	❏	Slovakia	❏
Azerbaijan	❏	Argentina	❏
Spain	❏	Nigeria	❏
Brazil	❏	Turkey	❏
Germany	❏	Finland	❏
Holland	❏	Croatia	❏
USA	❏	Albania	❏
Colombia	❏	Greece	❏
Denmark	❏	Iceland	❏
France	❏	Italy	❏
Mexico	❏		

```
S E Y K I S C V T H D C P A O
I X N W H D N D N N P O D I C
C Q E I H Q U I A I R L E R I
E A I K A V O L S T I O N T X
L O P E I R R E U I G M M S E
A S U T C E K G X N Y B A U M
N R A M Z N A U I E A I R A Y
D L G T P L A G K S K A K N A
Y I I E A Z E R B A I J A N I
A W W F N R U M F T G M N P T
S H N N I T L I Z A R B O S A
D D N A L N I F K E L L G P O
H O L L A N D N G U A B X A R
A L B A N I A X A N T V E I C
G R E E C E U Q D X Q F X N N
```

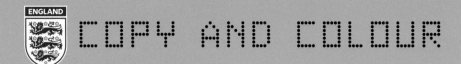

STEWART DOWNING

DOB: 22.07.84

Club: Middlesbrough

England Debut: England vs. Holland 02.05

Position in England Team: Midfielder

Appearances for England: 1

Goals Scored: 0

BIOGRAPHY:

Downing has been a revelation for Middlesbrough this year, with his sweet left foot upsetting many a Premiership defence. Having earned seven Under-21 England caps, Downing received the call from Eriksson to join the Senior squad against Holland in February 2005. Yet to start for the Senior team, Downing received his first cap as a substitute for Shaun Wright-Phillips.

DID YOU KNOW?

Stewart Downing isn't just a Middlesbrough player, he was born in the town and is a local hero.

STEWART DOWNING

England & Middlesbrough

ENGLAND CROSSWORD

CAN YOU COMPLETE THIS CROSSWORD USING THE CLUES BELOW?

HINT: ALL THE ANSWERS ARE IN THIS BOOK!

Across

2. The number of World Cup Final tournaments England has played in

6. The striker should score lots of these!

7. Alan _ _ _ _ _ _ _ was the first England player to be sent off in 1968

9. Cuthbert _ _ _ _ _ _ _ was the first ever England captain

10. The referee's assistant is sometimes called this

Down

1. He's the England Captain and also plays for Real Madrid

3. Peter _ _ _ _ _ _ _ . This goalkeeper holds the record for most caps received

4. Bobby _ _ _ _ _ _ _ _ . This player holds the record for scoring the most goals for England

5. This country has won the World Cup more times than any other

8. England drew 2-2 with this team on 4th September 2004

2.

3.

4.

5.

6.

7.

8.

9.

10.

EMILE HESKEY

DOB: 11.01.78

Club: Birmingham City

England Debut: England vs. Hungary 04.99

Position in England Team: Forward

Appearances for England: 43

Goals Scored: 5

BIOGRAPHY:

Heskey scored goals for fun for England's Under 21's and earned his first start for the full side a month before joining Liverpool for £11million from Leicester. Powerful, quick and capable of terrorising the strongest of defenders, he impressed the England coaches with his versatility. Happiest as an out and out striker, Heskey can also play down the left.

He completed a £6.25million move to Birmingham City in May 2004 and was brought back into the England squad for the World Cup qualifiers in March 2005.

DID YOU KNOW?

Heskey scored his first goal for England against Malta, way back in 2000.

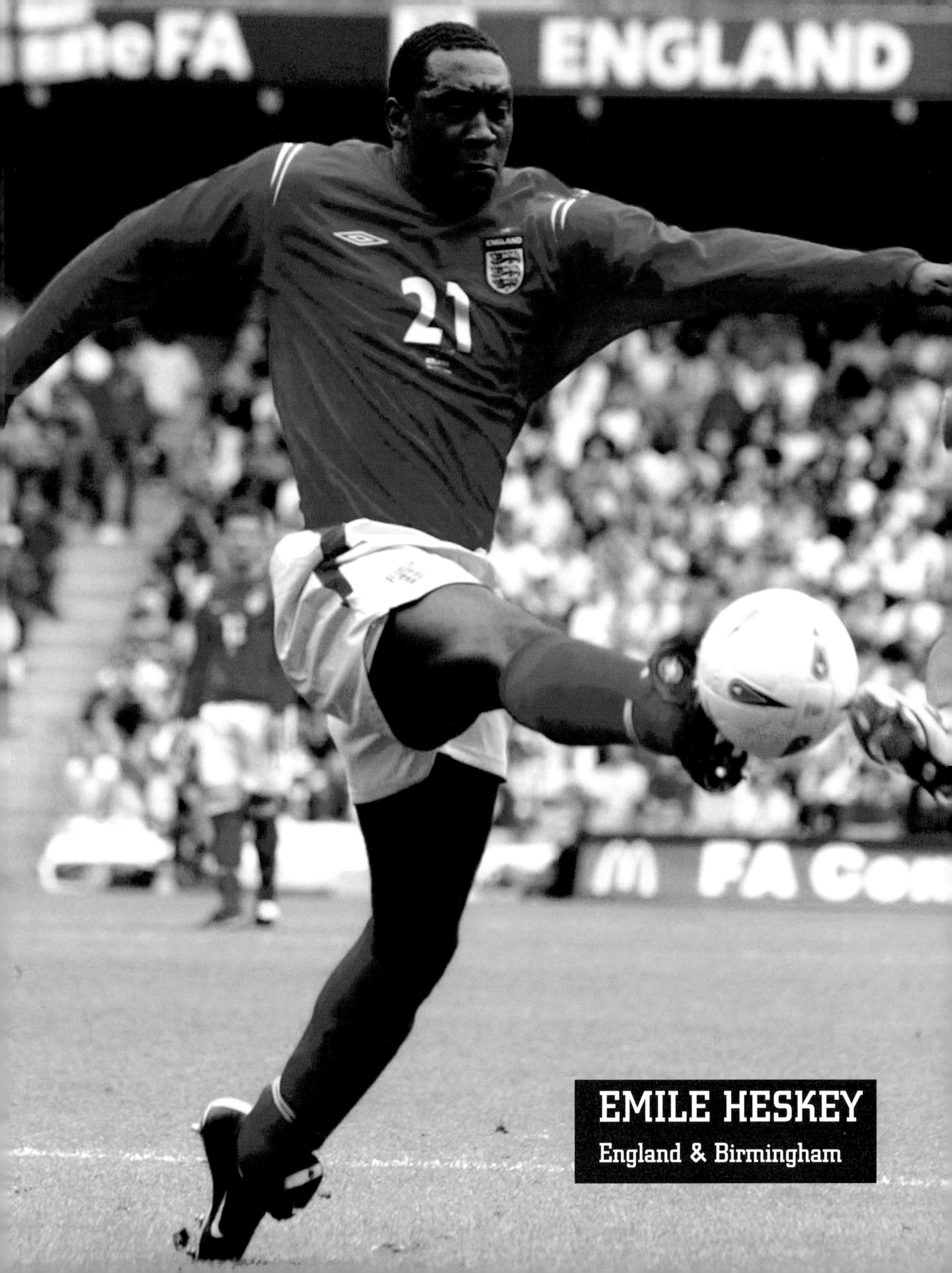

EMILE HESKEY
England & Birmingham

JERMAINE JENAS

DOB: 18.02.83

Club: Newcastle United

England Debut: England vs. Australia 02.03

Position in England Team: Midfielder

Appearances for England: 10

Goals Scored: 0

BIOGRAPHY:

Jenas, a talented youngster at Nottingham Forest who joined Newcastle as an 18-year-old, won nine caps at Under-21 level and progressed to make his full debut as a substitute against Australia in February 2003. Comfortable with the ball, Jenas looked increasingly at home at the top level as he made his first full England start in Azerbaijan last October.

DID YOU KNOW?

Jenas' second half performance against Australia earned him the Man of the Match award on his England debut.

JERMAINE JENAS
England & Newcastle Utd

WES BROWN

DOB: 13.10.79

Club: Manchester United

England Debut: England vs. Hungary 04.99

Position in England Team: Defender

Appearances for England: 8

Goals Scored: 0

BIOGRAPHY:

An accomplished central defender with a gift for reading the game, Brown was in fine form as he returned to the England starting line-up for 2005's February friendly with Holland.

The Manchester-born defender's career breakthrough came during the 1998-1999 season as he first gained a regular place in Sir Alex Ferguson's defence and then made his full England debut against Hungary in Budapest.

Injuries stalled Brown's international career but he soon returned to the squad for the 2002 World Cup finals.

DID YOU KNOW?

Wes Brown was a student at the prestigious FA National School.

WES BROWN
England & Man Utd

SVEN-GORAN ERIKSSON

BIOGRAPHY:

Sven joined England as coach of the national team in January 2001, having won the Italian league and cup double in 2000 with Lazio.

Eriksson's first game in charge was the 3-0 victory against Spain at Villa Park in a friendly international on 28th February 2001. Four subsequent wins in successive games meant that Sven had the most successful start of any England coach.

Under Sven, England qualified for the 2002 World Cup in one of the most dramatic campaigns in the Three Lions' history. Having reached the quarter-finals in Japan, the team qualified for Euro 2004 without losing a game. Again reaching the quarter-finals before losing to hosts Portugal on penalties, England and their coach are now looking ahead to the 2006 World Cup in Germany.

PAGE 12-13 CROSSWORD

Across	Down
2. World Cup	1. Lions
4. Eriksson	3. Lampard
7. Whistle	5. Hargreaves
8. Referee	6. Germany
10. Poland	7. White
11. Wembley	9. Moore
12. Yellow	13. Red
13. Rooney	

PAGE 20 SPOT THE BALL

Page 20 = D8

PAGE 21 SPOT THE BALL

Page 21 = G10

PAGE 24-25 CROSSWORD

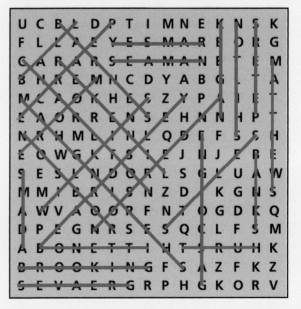

PAGE 30 FUN MAZE

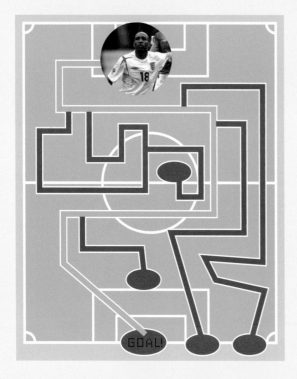

PAGES 38-39 WORDSEARCH

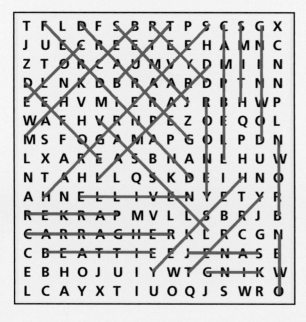

PAGE 42-43 SPOT THE DIFFERENCE

PAGE 58 JUMBLED WORDS

1. Anfield – Liverpool

2. Portman Road – Ipswich Town

3. St Mary's – Southampton

4. St James' Park – Newcastle United

5. Stamford Bridge – Chelsea

6. Villa Park – Aston Villa

7. Riverside – Middlesbrough

8. Old Trafford – Manchester United

PAGE 62 NUMBER PUZZLES

David Beckham

Wembley

Wayne Rooney

Frank Lampard

Old Trafford

PAGES 70-71 SPOT THE BALL

Page 70 = A9

Page 71 = B2

PAGES 74-75 WORDSEARCH

PAGES 80-81 CROSSWORD

Across	Down
2. Eleven	1. Beckham
6. Goals	3. Shilton
7. Mullery	4. Charlton
9. Ottaway	5. Brazil
10. Linesman	8. Austria

Show Your Colours!

On or off the pitch, make sure you've got the right kit!

Size 5 Signature Football
High quality PVC Football with all your favourite player's signatures.

Dream of England!
Your team's colours in curtains, duvet and pillowcases, beanbags, cushions and towels, all with the unmistakeable three lions badge.

Corinthian's England ProStars Blister Packs

Famous for their collectible football figurines, Corinthian's latest England release features ProStars of England heroes David Beckham, Steven Gerrard, Michael Owen and Frank Lampard. To purchase these and other England ProStars go to www.prostars.co.uk

Captain's Armband Set

Rubber ball, 500ml water bottle, mini pump, and captain's armband.

750ml Water Bottle

Plastic Shinguards

Goalkeeper Gloves

England Total Action Football

The great table top action game that recreates the excitement, pace and skill of a real International match! With magnetic action, each of the players can pass, shoot or trap the ball.

Storage Solutions

Affordable, durable storage for kids and adults alike. Light weight, collapsible and easy to clean ideal storage solutions for any England fan!

England Total Action Football available at all good toy shops. For further information, call Vivid Imaginations on 01702 200660. Bedroom items by Zap, available from all good high street stores and mail order companies including Argos, GUS, Toys R Us and Rosebys. Storage solutions by Wesco available from Shop Direct and Argos. For further information call the Wesco helpline on 0870 516 8194. Other items by Hy-Pro, available from JJB, Toys R Us, Toymaster and Woolworths or call 0870 402 1921 for your nearest stockist.